A *poem, "Little People," on the back cover of this book, begins with "A dreary place would be this earth, Were there no little people in it." With this in mind we, the following, are pleased to provide this gift entitled:*

"Four Seasons for Little People"

Dr. Timothy D. Reynolds - Family Dentistry

Cumberland Valley National Bank

Prudential - Don Foster Realtors

Connie Lawson - Broker/Owner

Richmond Wal-Mart Supercenter

Comfort Suites

Richmond Mall

YUASA

D1224410

Four Seasons for Little People

Text by
Dr. Jerry Ballard and daughter Kimberly Ballard
Illustrations by
Lynne Marie Davis

Special assistance from Greg Cherry, Chris Cherry, Merriana Branan and Leslie Underwood.

An Investment in the Future

A community's investment in education is an investment in its future. Business and professional leaders, as well as parents, should be partners with their schools. As a child's first and most influential teacher, parents play a monumental role in their education—a role which does not disappear when the child enters school. Parental involvement in their children's education contributes to improved student achievement, motivation and self-esteem. Parents who are active in their children's education expect more from schools and have positive attitudes toward schools and teachers.

Similarly, both parents, schools and the communities in which they reside gain when they support each other's aims.

A mutually supportive relationship among home, school and community contributes to the development of all, thus through such sharing strong partnerships result.

This book belongs to

_____

my name

This is my picture

_____

my teacher's name

_____

my school

For Parents and Teachers:

The purpose of this publication is to enhance and encourage the learning process in a fun way and to assist parents and teachers in their role as educators. Education holds the key to a better America. That is why business and professional leaders across the country are working in partnership with schools in providing this gift book to young children.

The reward these business and professional leaders receive is the satisfaction derived from making a worthwhile contribution to the development of future citizens in their community. If you agree and would like to see this program continued, please let those responsible know how much you appreciate their efforts. They are identified on the front page on this publication. Thank you for your support and your role in the educational process.

Publisher
Fidelity Associates, Inc.
2936 Rousseau Court
P.O. Box 3766
Gastonia, NC 28054-0020
Phone: 800-626-3766
www.fidelityassociates.com

Spring

Soon the days become a little longer and the sun a little warmer. It is Spring, the season of new life.

The warm sun awakens the sleeping seeds
and hiding animals.

Gentle rains bring
the green grass and
flowers back to life.

New leaves spring to
life on grand old trees
and tender new ones.

Spring is the season for
plowing and planting.

CORN

Baby birds and bunnies are born.
The earth awakens with living things.

It's time for playing outside
and enjoying fresh, clean air.
Feeling the warm sun on our face

We welcome back the singing birds.
We celebrate life.

Notes for Parents and Teachers: Spring

Spring begins when the sun's path crosses the earth's equator or center so that day and night have equal amounts of time all over the world. This occurs around March 21. Spring, then, is the three months from March 21 through June 20.

During spring, the snow and ice melt and rain falls, providing much-needed water for all the plants and animals that have slept all winter long. The sun shines, too, and that helps to feed the plants as they grow from tiny seeds into beautiful flowers or delicious vegetables. Trees bud and flower, and their leaves come back in bright green colors.

The wind in the spring is important, too. The wind blows seeds to the ground and bees spread pollen from flower to flower so things will grow. This is how the plants grow, the fields turn green, and the flowers bloom.

The return of the birds is another sign of spring. In March, millions of birds fly north, build their nests, and start new families

Everywhere, new life begins. Many animals give birth to their young during spring. Animals who grew thick coats for winter, like bears and foxes, horses and cows, shed them during the spring because it's much warmer outside. Sometimes birds use the discarded fur to make their nests more comfortable and sheltered from the wind.

Gardens grow and vegetables become ripe and ready to eat in spring and summer.

Spring makes everyone feel fresh and new. It is when nature rejoices, bringing beautiful, fragrant flowers, green grass, chirping birds, and baby animals. Celebrations during spring include Easter, the Passover and Mother's Day in May.

Summer

Summer is vacation time.
Enjoying the seashore.
Finding shells of all shapes and sizes.

Going fishing in safe,
sparkling waters,
which we work hard
to keep clean.

Swimming in the pool.

Playing barefoot./
Splashing in the rain.

The sun shines hot, giving little plants the light they need to grow.

Plants and trees and animals
are ours to protect.
They in turn provide for us.

Trees and plants give us material
to make things like clothes,
chairs, and paper to draw on.

Summer is a happy time to enjoy the earth and all it gives.

Notes for Parents and Teachers: Summer

Summer is the warmest time of the year, beginning June 21 and lasting until September 22. Two days after the beginning of summer, the sun reaches its highest point in the sky. That day is the longest day of the year, and the night is the shortest night.

During the summer, animals that plan to hibernate in the winter begin to eat a whole lot of food to store fat in their bodies. Bears especially eat a lot. Some animals in colder areas change color from shades of white in the winter to brown in the summer. This helps them blend with the season's colors and protects them from other animals.

Summer also means that school is out. In years past, farmers needed their children's help in the fields during the summer to prepare for Autumn harvest as well as tend the gardens that provided food during the summer. Now it is used as a time for vacation, bare feet, shorts, summer camp, and family time. We celebrate our country's birthday on July 4 with fireworks, parades and picnics. Fathers have a special day in June when we celebrate Father's Day.

Vegetables in the summer are the best! Fresh green beans, squash, butter beans, tomatoes, peas, carrots, potatoes, watermelons, cucumbers, lettuce, and many more. These vegetables also are harvested in the early Autumn.

Farmers harvest wheat during the summer. Wheat is one of our most important food sources. From wheat we make bread, cereal, spaghetti noodles, yummy cakes and cookies, and many other things to eat.

Summer time can get very hot. Longer, hotter days mean trips to the beach, mountains, rivers or lakes with the family. Building sand castles, swimming, sailing, fishing, exploring or just sun bathing can fill a long summer day. Cookouts at night with friends make the evenings special.

Other summer days can be filled with watching ladybugs and butterflies, making mud pies and searching for buried treasure or four leaf clovers. If you lie on a hill upside down and watch the clouds go by, you can almost feel the earth moving with you!

Autumn

Autumn also is called Fall.
Leaves change to beautiful colors before they fall to the ground.

glowing yellows,

Bright reds,

flaming oranges,

brilliant browns.

It's gathering time.
Farmers bring in food to
feed us during the winter.

And prepare their fields for next year's planting season.

Small animals gather nuts

and hide them for
the cold days ahead.

It is time for pumpkins, fall festivals and goodies of all kinds.

The full moon hangs low in the sky and looks very big.

The harvest moon.

We celebrate.
Families gather
to give thanks for
the earth's gifts.

And we go to school
to learn more about
life and living.

Notes for Parents and Teachers: Autumn

Autumn, the season of colors, starts on September 23 and lasts until December 21. When the air cools, tree leaves change from green to bright red, yellow and orange. Trees drop nuts and seeds to the ground allowing new trees to grow in the spring.

Autumn is a beautiful time of year, especially in the mountains where the colors are brightly displayed on rising land so you can see them all!

Apples and pears are favorite fruits for this time of year. And Autumn is the season of harvest because wheat, vegetables, fruit and nuts are all ready to be harvested for the final time of the year. Finishing touches on canning and freezing vegetables for winter are made. Pumpkin patches dot the countryside, and children search through the fields for the right pumpkin to take home.

Families come together in November to celebrate Thanksgiving. Thanksgiving began when the pilgrims shared their blessings and dinner with the Indians long ago. On Thanksgiving we eat lots of turkey and dressing and pumpkin pie for dessert. It is a day set aside to express gratitude for the many wonderful things we have.

Harvest moon falls on the night when the moon is so big and so bright you feel like you can almost touch it. Farmers can stay out in the fields and work longer. Festivals and dances are held to celebrate the harvest moon.

In September, we honor the millions of people who work each day by celebrating Labor Day. Many families take one last vacation during this holiday to enjoy the end of summer.

Later in Autumn the air gets cooler, leaves fall from trees and animals get sleepy and begin to grow thicker coats to prepare for winter. School starts and children make new friends and learn many new and interesting things.

Winter

Evenings become cooler.
The sun goes to bed earlier.
The trees are bare.
It is winter.

Time for warm coats
and mittens.

Watching the snow make
a winter wonderland.

Snuggling by the dancing, crackling fire.
Roasting marshmallows.

Grass and flowers sink
back into the ground
to wait for spring.

Gardeners cover the ground around their plants to keep them warm.

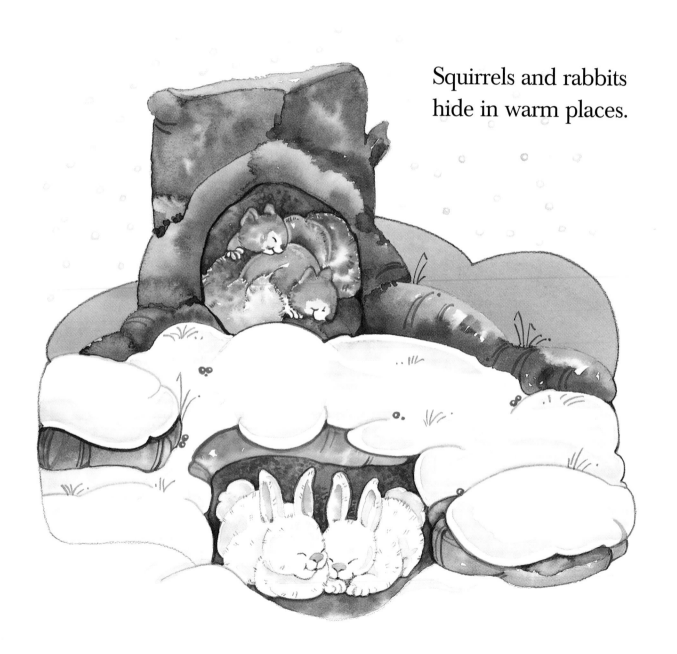

Squirrels and rabbits
hide in warm places.

Birds fly south to find warmer air.

Time to decorate the
Christmas tree and enjoy
the gifts of Christmas.

Days are short.

Nights are long.
Good time for reading stories
with our family.

Notes for Parents and Teachers: Winter

Winter is the coldest time of the year and lasts from December 22 until March 20. It is a time for overcoats, sweaters, and scarves. Lots of blankets are placed on the beds. Fires warm our homes.

In many places it snows. The air outside has to be colder than 32 degrees so that when it rains, the rain drops turn into snowflakes which blanket the yards, streets and houses. If it gets too cold, it will neither rain nor snow. And if the temperature stays around the low 30s, the rain might become ice and be dangerous to drive or play on.

If the snow gets really heavy and the wind becomes strong and blows the snow around, it is called a "blizzard," and snow can drift into high banks that look like white hills.

Snow can be great fun if you are bundled up well with warm clothes, boots and mittens or gloves. Building snowmen, sledding down hills, skiing, and throwing light snow balls at friends are all fun ways to spend snowy afternoons. Snow changes the scenery creating a bright winter wonderland. Snow helps farming, too, by covering the earth like a blanket to protect plants against the frost.

While you are playing hard outside, the rest of the life around you is sleeping. Squirrels are hibernating in the trees.

They sleep very deeply and their body temperature drops. If they've eaten all they should have in the summer and autumn, then their bodies have enough food to keep them from being hungry until they wake in the spring.

Bears, too, are said to hibernate but it's not real hibernation because their body temperature stays up and they wake up and walk around outside their homes on warmer winter days. And their cubs usually are born in the winter. Bears' coats, like the coats of horses, cows, foxes and other animals, grow very thick to keep them warm.

Most birds can't live in colder climates during the winter so they fly as far south as they can to stay warm. So animals have a choice in the winter. They can migrate (like birds do), they can hibernate (like squirrels do), or they can hide out in the ground or other safe places (like bears do).

Christmas, Hanukkah, and New Year's are favorite holidays. Schools close, and the streets are decorated with colorful lights.

Soon winter will melt into spring and heavy coats can be exchanged for warm sweaters. Birds will fly back, squirrels will wake up, and seeds that lay dormant all winter will begin to grow into fresh new plants.